Let's have a conversation about how the concepts in this book can be applied to your firm.

Please go to https://calendly.com/sue-tidswell to book time on my calendar.

Practically Brilliant Words of Wisdom on Hiring a High-Performing Sales Force

An Effective Hiring Process Is Essential to Your Sales Success

Sue Tidswell

THiNKaha®

An Actionable Business Journal

E-mail: info@thinkaha.com
20660 Stevens Creek Blvd., Suite 210
Cupertino, CA 95014

Please go to
http://aha.pub/EffectiveSalesForceHiring
to read this AHAbook and to share the
individual AHAmessages that resonate with you.

Published by THiNKaha®
20660 Stevens Creek Blvd., Suite 210,
Cupertino, CA 95014
http://thinkaha.com
E-mail: info@thinkaha.com

First Printing: November 2019
Hardcover ISBN: 978-1-61699-332-0   1-61699-332-4
Paperback ISBN: 978-1-61699-331-3   1-61699-331-6
eBook ISBN: 978-1-61699-333-7   1-61699-333-2
Place of Publication: Silicon Valley, California, USA
Paperback Library of Congress Number: 2019911408

Acknowledgements

I would like to acknowledge Terry Trayvick and Jorge Perez. Terry, without your guidance, belief in my potential, and demonstration of what true leadership is, I would not be the person I am today. Jorge, you continue to take me with you wherever you go, and I thank you for your trust and loyalty.

I have also been fortunate to work with an amazing HR team, Keri and Kelly, who are the Abbracci Group. These amazing people are part of my extended team. Thank you.

Finally, I would like to acknowledge Roy, Laura, and Tom, who are awesome sales leaders and friends. I have been fortunate to watch their careers develop and to see the amazing people they have become.

Dedication

I dedicate this book to my family because they have been my raison d'être.

Nick, I am so proud of your accomplishments. You did it your way and I know you are going to outsell them all.

How to Read a THiNKaha® Book

A Note from the Publisher

The AHAthat/THiNKaha series is the CliffsNotes of the 21st century. These books are contextual in nature. Although the actual words won't change, their meaning will every time you read one as your context will change. Be ready, you will experience your own AHA moments as you read the AHA messages™ in this book. They are designed to be stand-alone actionable messages that will help you think about a project you're working on, an event, a sales deal, a personal issue, etc., differently. As you read this book, please think about the following:

1. It should only take 15–20 minutes to read this book the first time out. When you're reading, write in the underlined area one to three action items that resonate with you.
2. Mark your calendar to re-read this book again in 30 days.
3. Repeat step #1 and mark one to three more AHA messages that resonate. They will most likely be different than the first time. BTW: this is also a great time to reflect on the AHA messages that resonated with you during your last reading.

After reading a THiNKaha book, marking your AHA messages, re-reading it, and marking more AHA messages, you'll begin to see how these books contextually apply to you. AHAthat/THiNKaha books advocate for continuous, lifelong learning. They will help you transform your AHAs into actionable items with tangible results until you no longer have to say AHA to these moments—they'll become part of your daily practice as you continue to grow and learn.

Mitchell Levy, The AHA Guy at AHAthat
publisher@thinkaha.com

THiNKaha®

Contents

Introduction

Selling today is highly complex. We are working in a world with sophisticated buyers who have as much access to information at their fingertips, or a call to Alexa, as we do. The salespeople we hire have to be disciplined in their processes, and they must seek to learn before they try to close a sale.

The characteristics of our new hires have evolved. Yes, they still need to be able to connect to people, but more than that, they have to be genuinely interested in the client and their business. They need to have the ability to engage, listen, understand, and create innovative solutions that truly bring value to the client.

Our salespeople need to be able to weave value propositions throughout their conversations with a potential client and not just deliver an elevator speech. A successful salesperson works in partnership with clients, allowing them to be coauthors of the solution and not just the recipient of a proposal. Finally, when hiring salespeople, they need to be team players. Whether it's with their peers or internal functions, they are not individual islands, and they will not have sustainable success over the long term if they cannot work with others.

Thinkables (a new Sue-ism) Prior to the Hiring Process

When thinking about sharing my sales leadership experience, my hope was that anyone reading it might learn a thing or two to make it worth their time. The biggest challenge was where to start. A wise person told me that I could not edit a blank sheet of paper, so I started with the beginning of the process: the hiring of great talent.

When do you know that you need to hire a salesperson? Is it when your goals are being increased, your existing team is at capacity, or you need to replace a non-performer? Before creating the job description for hiring a salesperson, I challenge you to answer the following questions:

1. Why do I need to hire a new salesperson?
2. Can this revenue be realized any other way?
3. When I find the right person, do I have the right opportunity for them?
4. Will this individual have the ability to grow revenue not only in the next six months and the next year but also over the next two years or more?
5. Is there a career of upward mobility, financially and personally, for the person? In a recent dialogue with a client, when hiring primarily millennials, the focus on the career conversation was key to keeping them engaged in the hiring process. So, make sure you have a career path that is mapped out that you can share.

Also, if you are seeking a replacement for non-performance, be sure to understand why the person failed. Be honest—get feedback from others if needed. Don't keep making the same mistake.

What experience are you looking for?

Entry-level positions: If hiring with minimal or no experience, make sure you have strong, hands-on leaders who can be in the field coaching and teaching. Remember that you get what you pay for, and it is not their fault if they fail due to lack of supervision. As for short-term goals, knowing the number they need to hit daily or weekly is a way to keep them focused and allows you to celebrate small wins. Motivate, motivate, motivate.

Experienced positions: The higher the goals and the margin, the greater the experience and the cost. So, think about the investment before you start the process. Payback may take longer, and the organization needs to be on board. People once given a well-planned-out onboarding program should be mostly self-directed, but they still need to be coached. Set up frequent communication sessions and pipeline calls to keep them on track and catch any challenges or issues early in their hiring. After three to four months, they should have built a strong pipeline with the ability to forecast future sales based on delivery and closing metrics.

What others are saying

When speaking with other sales leaders about hiring, we concurred that finding talent is becoming increasingly more challenging, especially since non-competes are in place to protect intellectual property, as in most industries. This often limits a company's ability to hire without restriction, except for states where a non-compete is non-binding. In addition, these people have a book of business on which they are being compensated, so how do you make the financial impact positive and not negative? My experience is to get creative without being unethical. It can and has been done.

In conclusion

Go slow to go fast in the hiring process. I have been put in the position to hire fast, but be assured you always repent in leisure. Do not be rushed to make the right decision; make sure that you have a 360-degree-view of the person, that you get that WOW factor after the interview, and that it is a cultural fit for them and you.

Sales is a number game; however, remember that quality is always above quantity and you need the art and the science. Achieve #SalesSuccess by having both hunters and farmers in your sales workforce. #EffectiveHiring

Sue Tidswell
http://aha.pub/EffectiveSalesForceHiring

Share the AHA messages from this book socially by going to
http://aha.pub/EffectiveSalesForceHiring.

Section I

The Value of Having a High-Performing Sales Force

Sales is what keeps businesses alive, and it's your sales force that drives sales for your business. Hiring high-performing salespeople is the key to your sales success. In *Good to Great*, Jim Collins describes getting the flywheel going in order to build momentum. In sales, you need to feel that every part of the team is effective and every new hire you make to your team will increase the velocity in which your team operates. In a high-performing sales force, you can feel the passion, the energy, and the excitement they bring as they move toward reaching their goals as individuals and as a group.

When hiring, you need to know what type of salespeople you need: do you need to hire hunters or farmers? You also need to determine the right match with your client, think of your clients first, and figure out what type of salesperson will connect with them the best. Once you know their needs, hire salespeople who will align to the criteria you have defined. By taking this step, you set the individual up for success, as they will more easily build strong relationships with your clients, and in addition, you set your business up for sales victory.

Watch this video:
http://aha.pub/SalesForceHiringS1

1

Your salespeople are the frontline of your brand to your prospects. If you want to close deals and achieve #SalesSuccess, hire a high-performing sales force to do the job. #EffectiveHiring

_____

_____

_____

2

To achieve #SalesSuccess, think about the value that hunters and farmers bring to your company and who to hire when. #EffectiveHiring

_____

_____

_____

3

Should you hire hunters or farmers? First, bring farmers to retain business. Once you've done that and have a secure base, you need hunters to grow the business.
#SalesSuccess #EffectiveHiring

_____

_____

_____

4

Hunters love winning something new and are motivated by having new clients, while farmers love the relationship and are motivated by supporting a client. Which are you looking for in your next sales hire?
#SalesSuccess #EffectiveHiring

_____

_____

_____

5

Retention by itself doesn't equal growth; the same goes for acquisition. You need both hunters and farmers to obtain growth, which equals the right amount of retention plus continued acquisition.
#SalesSuccess #EffectiveHiring

_____

_____

_____

6

Sales is a numbers game; however, remember that quality is always above quantity and you need both the art and the science. Achieve #SalesSuccess by having both hunters and farmers in your sales workforce. #EffectiveHiring

_____

_____

_____

7

Today, clients are well informed and may know as much about your product/service as others inside your company. As such, your salespeople need to be more sophisticated to cater to the needs of your clients. #SalesSuccess #EffectiveHiring

_____

_____

_____

8

Do you want #SalesSuccess? Talk to your clients first: Find out who they buy from and why. Who has won more of their business, and what were the qualities that the salesperson presented? #EffectiveHiring

_____

_____

_____

9

Have a clients-first-always focus. Being able to interpret and predict a client's needs is key. Business acumen should be one of the top things you consider when hiring. #SalesSuccess #EffectiveHiring

_____

_____

_____

10

Do you want to achieve #SalesSuccess?
Build client relationships with your best-in-class sales
force that are so good, they lead to referrals.
Set yourself up for sales tomorrow. #EffectiveHiring

_____

_____

_____

11

Sales is only part of the equation. It takes a salesperson
to sell the client, and it takes a team to keep them.
#SalesSuccess #HireEffectively

_____

_____

_____

High-performing salespeople are committed to understanding the broader needs of their prospects and keep the conversation going until they find the answer. #SalesSuccess #EffectiveHiring

Sue Tidswell
http://aha.pub/EffectiveSalesForceHiring

Share the AHA messages from this book socially by going to
http://aha.pub/EffectiveSalesForceHiring.

Section II

Characteristics of High-Performing Salespeople

How do you know you're hiring the "right" salespeople? Like any other profession, there are key traits you should look for when hiring a salesperson for your business. If you want sales success, you need to ensure that the salespeople you're hiring are bringing value to the table and are truly able to close deals.

In this section, you'll learn the different characteristics of high-performing salespeople and what you should look for in a sales hire. Hiring the right salespeople is a step forward to success for you and your business. There are derailers that you should look out for, those being traits that stop an individual from fulfilling their potential, which we often miss. Being an expert in the product, the market, or the technology and being highly impressive with insight might seem engaging, but not if they don't listen to their clients.

Watch this video:
http://aha.pub/SalesForceHiringS2

12

Characteristics of High-Performing Salespeople:
1) curious, 2) upbeat, 3) coachable, 4) accountable,
5) tech-savvy, 6) problem solver, 7) team player,
8) self-aware, 9) efficiently and ethically reach
their goals. #EffectiveHiring

_____

_____

_____

13

High-performing salespeople show up to the interview
equipped with lots of knowledge about the company
and are #Curious to learn more.
#SalesSuccess #EffectiveHiring

_____

_____

_____

14

A high-performing salesperson has already looked at your LinkedIn profile and website before they visit you, as a sign of respect. #SalesSuccess #EffectiveHiring

_____

_____

_____

15

High-performing salespeople are committed to understanding the broader needs of their prospects and keeping the conversation going until they find the answer. #SalesSuccess #EffectiveHiring

_____

_____

_____

16

High-performing salespeople that are #Curious win more, and more often, because no level is high enough for them. They are relentless when it comes to meeting and exceeding goals. #SalesSuccess #EffectiveHiring

_____

_____

_____

17

High-performing salespeople hear clients before they speak and don't rush to get to the revenue. They don't take shortcuts but instead, use data and tools available to them. #SalesSuccess #EffectiveHiring

_____

_____

_____

18

Have you ever been in a meeting with a salesperson where there was the ability to close the deal, but it didn't happen? High-performing salespeople listen to the prospect, stop talking, and close when appropriate. #SalesSuccess #EffectiveHiring

_____

_____

_____

19

Go slow to go fast. High-performing salespeople do their research and know their client before seeing them to earn their client's respect. #SalesSuccess #EffectiveHiring

_____

_____

_____

20

High-performing salespeople are #Curious.
They ask questions and listen to the answers.
#SalesSuccess #EffectiveHiring
http://aha.pub/SueTidswell-SalesHabits

_____

_____

_____

21

High-performing salespeople are both #Curious
and good listeners because if you're going to ask
questions to clients, you need to listen to their answers.
#SalesSuccess #EffectiveHiring

_____

_____

_____

22

High-performing salespeople don't sell; they show genuine concern about their client's business, and they get to know the person first and the business second. #SalesSuccess #EffectiveHiring

_____

_____

_____

23

High-performing salespeople are #Upbeat. They can't be glass half-empty, they need to be glass overflowing and be very positive thinking. #SalesSuccess #EffectiveHiring

_____

_____

_____

24

High-performing salespeople are never satisfied with their performance and want to achieve more. They show that they are #SelfAware and willing to learn. #SalesSuccess #EffectiveHiring

_____

_____

_____

25

High-performing salespeople need to be #Experts
(or have the ability to be experts) at understanding
the value of the products they bring.
#SalesSuccess #EffectiveHiring

_____

_____

_____

26

High-performing salespeople are coachable by their
sales leaders. They look for support to help them reach
their goals. #SalesSuccess #EffectiveHiring

_____

_____

_____

27

High-performing salespeople are #Accountable; they know their goals and own them. #SalesSuccess #EffectiveHiring

_____

_____

_____

28

A high-performing salesperson is #Responsible and takes initiative to stay on top of their work until they close a deal. #EffectiveHiring

_____

_____

_____

29

If the salesperson is not #TechSavvy, they can't do their research. If they can't do their research, they can't be successful. High-performing salespeople know how to use the latest tech in their sales strategy.
#SalesSuccess #EffectiveHiring

_____

_____

_____

30

High-performing salespeople are not just #Knowledgeable about the hard facts of your business, they are also knowledgeable about your company culture and whether it's right for them.
#SalesSuccess #EffectiveHiring

_____

_____

_____

31

High-performing salespeople efficiently and ethically reach their sales goals and quotas to achieve #SalesSuccess. #EffectiveHiring

_____

_____

_____

32

A sense of urgency is evident in high-performing salespeople, as they #Respond promptly and succinctly throughout the process to ensure they close. #SalesSuccess #EffectiveHiring

_____

_____

_____

33

It's not just about what a salesperson says—it's about how they say it. High-performing salespeople are just as interested in and excited about your company as your company is with them. #SalesSuccess #EffectiveHiring

_____

_____

_____

34

High-performing salespeople give a #Prompt response that demonstrates their interest in the company and position. #SalesSuccess #EffectiveHiring

_____

_____

_____

35

High-performing salespeople are financially-driven; they are good picture painters and are very #Passionate at what they do. #SalesSuccess #EffectiveHiring

_____

_____

_____

36

High-performing salespeople effectively #Communicate the value of your products or services to your clients to close deals. #EffectiveHiring

_____

_____

_____

37

High-performing salespeople do not just close deals; they continue adding value to clients, making repeat business, and earning client referrals. Do you want #SalesSuccess? #HireEffectively

_____

_____

_____

360° Process

Work with your HR partners to source the right assessment tools. If you want #SalesSuccess, leverage an HR expert to help with the #360 view of your prospective salespeople when hiring. #EffectiveHiring

Sue Tidswell
http://aha.pub/EffectiveSalesForceHiring

Share the AHA messages from this book socially by going to
http://aha.pub/EffectiveSalesForceHiring.

Section III

The 360 Process in Hiring Salespeople

There's no magic or shortcuts to hiring high-performing salespeople. To effectively hire good salespeople, businesses should look at the holistic view of your prospective salesperson.

This section discusses a 360 process in hiring salespeople. This defined process is constantly updated with hiring technologies and trends such as assessment tools that will make the search for the right salespeople more purposeful, insightful, transparent, and real. The key components are the initial interviews: the assessments, in-person interviews and/or presentations, and finally, the internal team review. Many companies use assessment tools, but for those who don't, this section should provide insight into why they are important.

Watch this video:
http://aha.pub/SalesForceHiringS3

38

There's no shortcut to finding high-performing salespeople. The #360 process provides a multidimensional level of recruitment insight that leads to #EffectiveHiring and #SalesSuccess.

_____

_____

_____

39

The more consistent the sales process, the better we get at hiring. #SalesSuccess #EffectiveHiring

_____

_____

_____

40

In today's world with AI and info at our fingertips, we should use our intuition, assessment tools, and inclusion of insight from functional peers to make a #360 informed decision faster. #SalesSuccess #EffectiveHiring

_____

_____

_____

41

Hiring a salesperson requires you to be intuitive, but you need to road-test the facts in #360 to ensure #EffectiveHiring. #SalesSuccess

_____

_____

_____

42

Assessment tools provide a holistic view of the salespeople you're hiring to help determine if they have the energy, passion, and drive to achieve #SalesSuccess. #EffectiveHiring

_____

_____

_____

43

Assessment tools will provide insight into how the salesperson can be coached and whether they are team players. #SalesSuccess #EffectiveHiring

_____

_____

_____

44

Work with your HR partners to source the right assessment tools. If you want #SalesSuccess, leverage an HR expert to help with the #360 view of your prospective salespeople when hiring. #EffectiveHiring

_____

_____

_____

45

Before opening up the requirement for a salesperson, ask questions such as: What are the expectations? What's stopping the salesperson from achieving those results? #360 #SalesSuccess #EffectiveHiring

_____

_____

_____

46

When you get down to the top 2–3 candidates, use an assessment tool to tell if they are good hunters or not.
#360 #SalesSuccess #EffectiveHiring

_____

_____

_____

47

From the hiring process, work with HR to determine if they fit into the company culture.
#360 #SalesSuccess #EffectiveHiring

_____

_____

_____

48

When hiring a salesperson, ask a lot of questions and understand the differences in their approach under different scenarios. #360 #SalesSuccess #EffectiveHiring

_____

_____

_____

49

In order to test a prospective salesperson's resilience, use measurement tools that show you a #360 angle on how they handle clients, so you have a good idea if they can achieve #SalesSuccess. #EffectiveHiring

_____

_____

_____

50

Ask prospective salespeople to give an example of something that took a short amount of time vs. a long one. What were they selling, who was the client, and what was the difference in the sales cycle? #360 #SalesSuccess #EffectiveHiring

_____

_____

_____

51

When you're hiring a previously successful salesperson, look at the sales approach they have used in the past, align what they were doing with what you want to have done, and together, you will make 2+2 =5. #360 #SalesSuccess #EffectiveHiring

_____

_____

52

For salespeople to be effective, you should be instrumental in helping them get up to speed and understand the true value of your products/services.
#360 #SalesSuccess #EffectiveHiring

_____

_____

_____

53

When hiring a salesperson, get the onboarding/training done in the first two weeks.
#360 #SalesSuccess #EffectiveHiring

_____

_____

_____

54

#EffectiveHiring means setting expectations right from the start, like how many calls, proposals, and presentations the salesperson will make to get to discovery and close. #360 #SalesSuccess

_____

_____

_____

55

When interviewing a salesperson, both sides should set expectations of what's real and what's not. If you get it wrong in the hiring process, you'll get it wrong the entire way. #360 #SalesSuccess #EffectiveHiring

_____

_____

_____

56

When interviewing a prospective salesperson, set expectations (pipeline in first three months, first sale, total revenue in year one) and ask them if it's realistic. If so, how would they go about doing that? #360 #SalesSuccess #EffectiveHiring

_____

_____

_____

57

When interviewing a salesperson, ask what they are most passionate about and what they are least passionate about and why?
#360 #SalesSuccess #EffectiveHiring

_____

_____

_____

58

When hiring a salesperson, look for someone who is committed to continuous learning and self-improvement.
#360 #SalesSuccess #EffectiveHiring

_____

_____

_____

59

When hiring a salesperson, find out about their business and personal goals and what they want to achieve. #360 #SalesSuccess #EffectiveHiring

_____

_____

_____

60

High-performing salespeople plan their: 1) number of calls, 2) number of proposals, 3) hours spent for clients, 4) target completion date, and 5) expected revenue. #360 #SalesSuccess #EffectiveHiring

_____

_____

_____

61

Setting expectations from the get-go is key to hiring a successful salesperson. #SalesSuccess #EffectiveHiring

_____

_____

_____

62

When you're down to the final two sales candidates, ask both to do research and present to you and an internal team, like they would to a client. #SalesSuccess #EffectiveHiring

_____

_____

_____

63

Do not be rushed to make the salesperson hire; make sure you have a #360 view that ensures a cultural fit and an ability to work with other areas of the company. #SalesSuccess #EffectiveHiring

_____

_____

_____

When a salesperson and the entire organization embrace each other, you not only maximize the resources that you have, you also #EffectivelyHire and increase chances of #SalesSuccess. #Inclusivity

Sue Tidswell
http://aha.pub/EffectiveSalesForceHiring

Share the AHA messages from this book socially by going to
http://aha.pub/EffectiveSalesForceHiring.

Section IV

Inclusive Decision Making

Culture trumps all. When you include other members of your organization in the decision-making process, it helps ensure that you hire salespeople who will truly contribute to both sales and the overall business.

Practicing inclusive decision making not only ensures that you hire effectively, but it also ensures that you make other people in your organization truly feel like a part of it. And when prospective salespeople see the value you place on everyone in your team, they will want to work with you and help you (and the organization) achieve success.

Watch this video:
http://aha.pub/SalesForceHiringS4

64

Sales is one of the most transparent positions of the company, and success (both good and bad) is there for all to judge. #EffectivelyHire and help the salesperson achieve #SalesSuccess. #Inclusivity

_____

_____

_____

65

Having a #360 view of your entire sales team is key. You want all points of input to achieve #SalesSuccess. #EffectiveHiring

_____

_____

_____

66

Everyone in your organization owns the client.
If you want #SalesSuccess, have your organization
know they are all accountable to the client and
to provide the best service they can in their role.
#Inclusivity #EffectiveHiring

_____

_____

_____

67

Including other functions in the decision making
helps set up salespeople for
#SalesSuccess. #Inclusivity #EffectiveHiring

_____

_____

_____

68

A salesperson can work better if they have met and interacted with other people in the organization. Do you practice #Inclusivity? #SalesSuccess #EffectiveHiring

_____

_____

_____

69

When a salesperson and the entire organization embrace each other, you not only maximize the resources that you have, you also #EffectivelyHire and increase chances of #SalesSuccess. #Inclusivity

_____

_____

_____

70

When a salesperson has met others in the organization and has been embraced, they will want to work with you. #Inclusivity #EffectiveHiring

_____

_____

_____

71

Set up a process where key functions in the organization can evaluate the salesperson on a scale of 1–5 to see if the salesperson fits in. #Inclusivity #EffectiveHiring

_____

_____

_____

72

Have the organization vote, review the assessment tool results, and evaluate the presentation the salesperson will give. #Inclusivity #EffectiveHiring

_____

_____

_____

73

What does someone in operations look for in evaluating a sales hire? They look for those who will deliver in alignment with the operations team's #SalesSuccess. Look for the same. #Inclusivity #EffectiveHiring

_____

_____

_____

74

What does someone in branding look for in evaluating a sales hire? They look for a person who represents the brand of the company. Look for the same.
#Inclusivity #EffectiveHiring

_____

_____

_____

75

What does someone in finance look for in evaluating a sales hire? They look for a person who can negotiate, bring value, and sell the products at a good margin. Look for the same. #Inclusivity #EffectiveHiring

_____

_____

_____

76

What does someone in HR look for in evaluating a sales hire? They look for a person who's empathetic enough to work across different functions. Look for the same. #Inclusivity #EffectiveHiring

_____

_____

_____

77

What does someone in marketing look for in evaluating a sales hire? They look for a person who understands what the product will do for a client. Look for the same. #Inclusivity #EffectiveHiring

_____

_____

_____

78

What do other salespeople look for in evaluating a sales hire? They look for a person who's individually competitive while also being a team player. #Inclusivity #EffectiveHiring

_____

_____

_____

79

What does someone in executive leadership look for in evaluating a sales hire? They look at the person's potential, if they fit culturally, and if they bring value to the organization's #SalesSuccess. #Inclusivity #EffectiveHiring

_____

_____

_____

80

Chances of hiring a high-performing salesperson that closes deals is low if you don't have everyone in your organization participate in the hiring process.
#Inclusivity #EffectiveHiring

_____

_____

_____

81

To ensure that your salespeople perform well and close deals, be the bridge that connects your salespeople to other members of your organization.
#Inclusivity #EffectiveHiring

_____

_____

_____

82

The salesperson presents your brand to clients. Can they communicate the way you want your brand communicated in the marketplace? Hearing the thoughts of everyone in your organization helps you #EffectivelyHire a salesperson. #Inclusivity

_____

_____

_____

When #ClosingTheDeal, what are the key reasons they will choose to work with you? When you determine the reason, give them what they want so they can achieve #SalesSuccess. #EffectiveHiring

Sue Tidswell
http://aha.pub/EffectiveSalesForceHiring

Share the AHA messages from this book socially by going to
http://aha.pub/EffectiveSalesForceHiring.

Section V

Closing the Deal

Closing the deal should be the toughest part of the sales hiring process. It's important to have market data to know where to start the negotiation and what is competitive. It's important to ascertain throughout your dialogue what drives the salesperson and why they would leave their current position to work for you.

Offering incentives and opportunities to earn "lots of money" are what attract and drive highly successful salespeople. But it's more than just "money." If you want to hire and keep high-performing salespeople, ensure that you offer them what they deserve, which also includes status, recognition, and career mobility. This section takes you through the questions and provides insight to ready you for negotiation.

Watch this video:
http://aha.pub/SalesForceHiringS5

83

High-performing salespeople are on you (in a good way) all the time. They want to stretch the system, and they have the energy and the passion, you just need to fuel it. #ClosingTheDeal #EffectiveHiring

_____

_____

_____

84

When you #CloseTheDeal, make sure you sit down and negotiate the offer. Determine what they want to earn. #EffectiveHiring

_____

_____

_____

85

When it's time to hire, the sales leader becomes the salesperson selling the candidate and negotiating to #CloseTheDeal. #EffectiveHiring

_____

_____

_____

86

It's really important to understand the key drivers that motivate the salesperson. Why would they want to join you? #ClosingTheDeal #EffectiveHiring

_____

_____

_____

87

Is the salesperson "really" looking, or are they looking for an offer so they can renegotiate with their current company? #ClosingTheDeal #EffectiveHiring

_____

_____

_____

88

When #ClosingTheDeal, what are the key reasons the salesperson will choose to work with you? When you determine the reason, give them what they want so they can achieve #SalesSuccess. #EffectiveHiring

_____

_____

_____

89

So many people want to hire salespeople and cap what they earn, and that's wrong. The more sales the person brings in, the better. #PayThem! #ClosingTheDeal #EffectiveHiring

_____

_____

_____

90

When you're hiring salespeople, do you know what the market rates are and what your competitors are paying? Understand the total compensation the salesperson is interested in earning. When #ClosingTheDeal, it's the sales leader's time to sell. #EffectiveHiring

_____

_____

_____

91

When hiring salespeople, let them know up front that there's a rewards program. It doesn't matter what it is, it's an ability to earn status. #ClosingTheDeal #EffectiveHiring

_____

_____

_____

92

Incentives drive salespeople. If you want the salesperson to think of nothing but #SalesSuccess, apply gamification. Make sure they are recognized when they're successful.
#ClosingTheDeal #EffectiveHiring

_____

_____

_____

93

Encourage top salespeople to use LinkedIn to promote their abilities, as clients view profiles too. #ClosingTheDeal #EffectiveHiring

_____

_____

_____

94

Being selected to be a mentor to others is great recognition for a salesperson. If the person they mentored meets their goals, they get paid as well. It's a win-win. #ClosingTheDeal #EffectiveHiring

_____

_____

_____

95

Give rewards to top salespeople. Host an annual retreat. In smaller companies, give an extra bonus, dinner with the CEO, or a weekend away with the spouse. #ClosingTheDeal #EffectiveHiring

_____

_____

_____

96

Want to #EffectivelyHire salespeople? Give recognition, status, ego, and money when they deserve it. Do you have the right stuff in your mix? #ClosingTheDeal

_____

_____

_____

Inspect whom your salespeople are selling to, what conversations they are having, and if they are closing business.
#InspectWhatYouExpect #EffectiveHiring

Sue Tidswell

http://aha.pub/EffectiveSalesForceHiring

Share the AHA messages from this book socially by going to
http://aha.pub/EffectiveSalesForceHiring.

Section VI

Inspect What You Expect

The key to generating more sales revenue is setting short-term and long-term goals for your salespeople, proactively tracking and monitoring processes and methodologies until your salespeople produce skyrocketing results. To do this, sales leaders need to be proactive, they need to assign tasks, and they need to coach, mentor, and work with the salespeople to reach their goals.

Working closely with salespeople and providing constructive feedback in the moment helps motivate and drive salespeople to perform and exceed expectations. After all, salespeople need all the support they can get to attain sales quotas and revenue goals that are never easy.

Watch this video:
http://aha.pub/SalesForceHiringS6

97

Hiring the salesperson is the first step in the process; ensuring their success is what comes next. What do you do after hiring? #InspectWhatYouExpect #EffectiveHiring

_____

_____

_____

98

Feedback is a gift. The continuous learning and development of your salespeople is priceless. #InspectWhatYouExpect #EffectiveHiring

_____

_____

_____

99

Effective mentoring means helping your sales force get better and be twice as efficient as they already are. #InspectWhatYouExpect #EffectiveHiring

_____

_____

_____

100

When you hire someone, you must realize that they are not autonomous. Working with others in your team is key to their integration.
#InspectWhatYouExpect #EffectiveHiring

_____

_____

_____

101

Salespeople are like any high-performing athlete: They need to be coached, directed, mentored, and provided constructive feedback for them to meet and exceed their goals. #InspectWhatYouExpect #EffectiveHiring

_____

_____

_____

102

Reinforce ongoing sales training. For your salespeople to achieve #SalesSuccess, help them focus on self-development. #InspectWhatYouExpect #EffectiveHiring

_____

_____

_____

103

Understand how a salesperson is best coached and how to maximize their potential. Leverage the feedback from assessment tools used in the hiring process. #InspectWhatYouExpect #EffectiveHiring

_____

_____

_____

104

Inspect whom your salespeople are selling to, what conversations they are having, and if they are closing business. #InspectWhatYouExpect #EffectiveHiring

_____

_____

_____

105

Make sure that both you and the salesperson you hire know what is being inspected. To drive success for the candidate, create a plan for success, then measure and analyze it. #InspectWhatYouExpect #EffectiveHiring

_____

_____

_____

106

To achieve #SalesSuccess, show your salespeople what they need to do to make X amount of money. Doing quantitative inspection will help find the "repeatable" methodology that works. #InspectWhatYouExpect #EffectiveHiring

_____

_____

_____

107

Activity alone does not a successful salesperson make. You can't coach just on activities. Activity by itself doesn't drive results. #InspectWhatYouExpect #EffectiveHiring

_____

_____

_____

108

Measure results, not activity.
Activity provides insight into trends and skills.
#InspectWhatYouExpect. #EffectiveHiring

_____

_____

_____

109

Questions to Determine What to Expect:
1) Are the activities producing results?
2) Are the conversations leading to the right outcomes?
3) Are you doing it in an efficient and effective way?
#InspectWhatYouExpect #EffectiveHiring

_____

_____

_____

110

Monitor the salesperson during the onboarding process to ensure that they will pass the first 90 days.
#InspectWhatYouExpect #EffectiveHiring

_____

_____

_____

111

The onboarding process is key to making a successful salesperson. Do you have an effective onboarding process? You should! #InspectWhatYouExpect #EffectiveHiring

_____

_____

_____

112

If you don't have a good onboarding process, you won't keep your good salespeople because you're not helping them to be successful. #InspectWhatYouExpect #EffectiveHiring

_____

_____

_____

113

In the onboarding process, be clear on
what is expected. What is the market plan?
Who is your salesperson going to sell to?
#InspectWhatYouExpect #EffectiveHiring

_____

_____

_____

114

Walk your prospective salesperson through the
entire sales process, and let them know how
you are going to evaluate their performance.
#InspectWhatYouExpect #EffectiveHiring

_____

_____

_____

115

What's your salespeople's plan to achieve what is expected? What's going to make the plan happen? Have a coaching dialogue to help the salesperson reach their goals. #InspectWhatYouExpect #EffectiveHiring

_____

_____

_____

116

Sales leaders need to coach and teach salespeople.
You get what you pay for; it's not your salespeople's
fault if they fail due to lack of supervision.
#InspectWhatYouExpect #EffectiveHiring

_____

_____

_____

117

What do salespeople want?
They want sales leaders who can give better insight
into their business and help them achieve
#SalesSuccess. #InspectWhatYouExpect #EffectiveHiring

_____

_____

_____

118

Do you have enough sales coaching and training being done in your organization today?
If not, is this something you can fix?
#InspectWhatYouExpect #EffectiveHiring

_____

_____

_____

119

Sales leaders can easily see talent shortage in an organization, so they're always on the lookout to fill the gap by moving salespeople up and encouraging leaders to rise up. #InspectWhatYouExpect #EffectiveHiring

_____

_____

_____

120

High-performing sales leaders don't just manage; they provide a roadmap of execution to build a quality sales force that exceeds targets and sales quotas. What kind of sales leaders do you have? #InspectWhatYouExpect #EffectiveHiring

_____

_____

_____

121

The sales leader lets the salesperson know why they should put their activity in the CRM. It's to help the salesperson be successful. #SalesSuccess #EffectiveHiring

_____

_____

_____

122

The sales leader needs to work very closely with their salespeople to know where they are, what they are doing, and how the sales leader can help. Continuous review of the necessary elements is key to success! #SalesSuccess #EffectiveHiring

_____

_____

_____

123

Sales leaders need to have the processes and structure in place for the salespeople to know their target markets and goals and have the processes in place to achieve them. #InspectWhatYouExpect #EffectiveHiring

_____

_____

_____

124

The weekly sales conversation is typically done with the CRM. High-performing sales leaders say, "This is what I see as your pipeline, is that correct?" #InspectWhatYouExpect #EffectiveHiring

---

125

If a salesperson is not delivering results, a good sales leader will look at their activities to see what needs to happen to deliver results. #InspectWhatYouExpect #EffectiveHiring

---

126

Good sales leaders are always coaching. They must be a coach 24x7 and conduct 1x1s weekly, starting from Day 1. #InspectWhatYouExpect #EffectiveHiring

_____

_____

_____

127

Good sales leaders look at both the quantitative and qualitative measurements of success. They're not just a success coach to the salesperson, they're also an accountability coach. #InspectWhatYouExpect #EffectiveHiring

_____

_____

_____

128

Companies need to train sales leaders on how to be good coaches to their people. Is this an active program you have in your organization? #InspectWhatYouExpect #EffectiveHiring

_____

_____

_____

129

What most companies should have to make their revenue growth targets is a strong sales leader who's also a coach and mentor to their salespeople. #InspectWhatYouExpect #EffectiveHiring

_____

_____

_____

130

Every organization's revenue can dramatically increase if only sales leaders help educate their salespeople by coaching them to achieve sales success. #InspectWhatYouExpect #EffectiveHiring

_____

_____

_____

External recruiters have the knowledge, experience, and insight to ask the right questions of your future sales leaders and salespeople to identify those who will be great.
#SalesSuccess #EffectiveHiring

Sue Tidswell

http://aha.pub/EffectiveSalesForceHiring

Share the AHA messages from this book socially by going to
http://aha.pub/EffectiveSalesForceHiring.

Section VII

Having an External Sales Hiring Firm

It takes time to know whether a sales candidate is a good fit for the culture of your business and if their core values align with yours. Effective sales force hiring not only takes a lot of time, but it also takes sound experience and knowledge. You need to know the filters that streamline the lengthy process of getting sales candidates to the final step.

Ensuring that both parties are getting what they want and communicating the true expectations is what an external sales hiring firm does best. By having a third-party perspective of your business and salespeople, an external sales hiring firm can help lead you to an effective and successful sales hiring process.

Watch this video:
http://aha.pub/SalesForceHiringS7

131

Benefits of having an external recruiter: 1) They look at the sales process in a different perspective, and 2) they help the salesperson and sales leaders see what they're not doing and where they are not selling.
#SalesSuccess #EffectiveHiring

_____

_____

_____

132

To make a sales hire, the typical internal recruiter needs to review an average of at least 64 resumes -> 30 conversations -> 15 follow-ups -> 5 top candidates -> 3 to interview. Save time by hiring an external sales hiring firm. #SalesSuccess #EffectiveHiring

_____

_____

_____

133

Internal recruiters usually don't have a network of sales people in their database, and it can take time to get to the right people. #SalesSuccess #EffectiveHiring

---

134

Internal recruiters can source, but this adds a step in the process to #SalesSuccess. Their true cost is not free, and they may still not put the "right" candidates in your organization. #EffectiveHiring

---

135

External recruiters have the knowledge, experience, and insight to ask the right questions of your future sales leaders and salespeople to identify those who will be great. #SalesSuccess #EffectiveHiring

_____

_____

_____

136

External recruiters look for the how and why sales coaching is required to be successful.
Are you creating a successful sales environment?
#SalesSuccess #EffectiveHiring

_____

_____

_____

137

External recruiters can save your organization the pain
of finding a hunter who finds you a "real buyer"
and doesn't stop until they get you one.
#SalesSuccess #EffectiveHiring

_____

_____

_____

138

External recruiters help you grow your pipeline quickly, and they coach others in your organization as well. #SalesSuccess #EffectiveHiring

_____

_____

_____

139

By hiring external recruiters, you can decrease the ramp-up time, which will result in more sales for your organization quicker. #HiringEffectively. #SalesSuccess

_____

_____

_____

140

It takes time and effort to hire people, particularly the "right" person. If there's a firm to outsource that, it frees up the team to focus on what's more relevant. #SalesSuccess #EffectiveHiring

_____

_____

_____

Appendix A

Coaching Them to Success

Hiring the salesperson is the first step in the process; ensuring their success is what comes next. Salespeople are like any high-performing athlete: they need to be coached, directed, mentored, and provided constructive feedback in order for them to meet and exceed their goals. It is important, however, to understand how a salesperson is best coached and to know how to maximize their potential. The easiest way to do this is to leverage the feedback from the Assessment Tool used in the hiring process. The investment made equips the sales leader and their HR partner with invaluable knowledge of how best to motivate and develop the salesperson. You will find that once hired, providing feedback and insight to the salesperson based on their assessment is a way to get them started and feeling that you are truly interested in them. I have yet to meet a salesperson who does not want to know what their assessment revealed.

There are various assessment programs in the market, but the three I have had the most exposure to are Wonderlic, Caliper, and HBDI (Hermann Brain Dominance Instrument). I select one of these based on the level of sales for which I am hiring and the length of the sales cycle. I segment sales into two categories:

1. Transactional Sales: The individuals hired for this type of business need to be comfortable with cold calling and making hundreds of connections, have a high rejection tolerance, are goal driven, have perseverance, and don't mind repetition. The sales cycle is typically short and commissions paid on a more frequent basis. For these roles, I usually use Wonderlic, as it is an efficient and effective tool and does not intimidate the candidate. https://www.wonderlic.com

2. Solution Sales: Solution selling requires greater relationship-building skills, problem solving, risk assessment, teamwork, and attention to detail. Sales cycles are longer and goals take longer to achieve and compensation slower to realize, but the reward is higher. Caliper probes deeper into the intellect and intelligence of the person; it takes longer and is more intense. Knowing more about this level of salesperson is critical for you to be confident that they can be successful. www.calipercorp.com

For coaching and development, HBDI is my go-to for knowing how salespeople prefer to think, how they receive information, what drives them, and most importantly, how they interface with others, especially clients. It is simple and based on using red, blue, yellow, and green colors to identify brain quadrants and a person's preferred way of thinking. All the teams I have led go through this process so I know how to coach them and how they will best work together as a team. I once had 125 salespeople wearing their preferred color badge at a national sales meeting, and it created more conversations than I ever thought possible. By the way, my most successful salespeople were a combination of yellow, blue, and red. https://ww.herrmannsolutions.com.

My advice when using any of these applications is to ensure that your HR team is involved. First, you want to make sure that your approach and reasoning is well-thought-out. Second, as this becomes part of their ongoing development, the individual should know that the organization is investing in them and their future. If you are like me and don't have access to an in-house HR team, Abbracci Group is a specialized HR company that I use and recommend if you need further insight in making this part of your sales hiring and development process. https:// abbraccigroup.com/

Feedback is a gift, and continuous learning and development of our salespeople and teams is priceless.

Appendix B

Green Flags

When You Know You Want to Hire This One

In his book, *Blink*, Malcolm Gladwell says, "Your unconscious is the world's fastest filter of information," and that our intuition is often right. In today's world, with AI and information at our fingertips, we can use that amazing intuition and add data to make informed decisions faster.

Hiring a salesperson requires you to be intuitive but to also road test the facts. When I find a salesperson who feels right and can pass the Formula One test drive (aka the interview), then I know we are ready to go to the starting line together.

1. They know "your stuff," not just "their stuff"

When it comes to knowledgeable salespeople, I appreciate those who have done their research on the company and the position in advance—they have done their homework. It shows that they have the right habits and tend to be better culture fits, come in with the right expectations, and be able to get ramped up more quickly.

An ideal salesperson shows up to the interview equipped with knowledge about the company and curious to learn more. It's obvious when a salesperson has really done their research and taken the time to know who the company is before their interview. This demonstrates that they can be self-directed and are genuinely interested in the position.

Culture eats strategy for breakfast, and a salesperson shouldn't just be knowledgeable about the hard facts of your business; they should also be knowledgeable about your company culture and whether it's right for them.

2. They are excited and have positive energy

When you meet someone for the first time and they have an aura about them, an energy and enthusiasm, everything they say is positive and you know you like this person. It's not just about what a salesperson says—it's about how they say it. The right salesperson should be just as interested and excited about your company as your company is about them, and if you can see that in their body language and hear it in their voice, it's a great sign.

3. They are open, honest, and have learned from experience

We are all searching for the ideal salesperson, but the truth is, no one is perfect. So, having a salesperson who is willing to identify their imperfections is great. When they can share their weaknesses or identify an area of development, they are showing that they are willing to be open and honest and trust that you will not judge them. Examples of learning show character, and when a salesperson can share their losses, as well as their wins, and can "own" their results, you know that they are genuine.

4. They have a sense of urgency
One of the most challenging parts of hiring a salesperson is simply the coordination. Scheduling phone meetings, interviews, and presentations between so many different schedules is tough, especially if the salesperson does not have a sense of urgency. This ability is evident in the best salespeople, as they respond promptly and succinctly throughout the process because they are keen to close this deal too.

When you are recruiting for a sales role, the time is now and it is fast-paced, and if prospective candidates are unmotivated to respond quickly during the recruitment process, they are less likely to be responsive once they are on the job. A prompt response demonstrates their interest in the company and position.

5. You just had a great conversation
When you leave the interview thinking that you just had a great conversation and came away with all your questions answered, you know this could be the one.

An interview that goes overtime but no one is looking at their watch shows that the dialogue was mutually engaging and that all parties had something of value to say. If you left the room wanting to have another conversation with the person and felt that they really did "fit in," this is a sure "green light."

6. Plan ahead
When the salesperson turns up with a 30-60-90-day plan, you know that you have likely hit the jackpot, especially if all the other components are in order. Coming to the interview with concrete ideas of what they would do in the role shows that a salesperson both understands the work well and wants to contribute as soon as they can.

Finally, it's essential for a salesperson to have a plan or proven record of success, be a team player, and know how to have a great conversation, but they also need to be able to think out of the box. The special ingredient for me is "innovation." Can they innovate and turn ideas into reality? When you have these six key ingredients, plus the special ingredient, you say *yes*.

Red Flags

When interviewing a sales candidate, you need to be tuned into the details because if they are good at what they do, which is sell, they might just try to charm their way into being hired. Don't be fooled—stay focused and make sure you are leading the conversation. Here are a few "red flags" to watch out for in the process.

Are they late for a very important date?
Did they arrive on schedule? (This is actually ten minutes before the interview in order to have enough time to collect their thoughts and breathe for a minute.) I look for a person who has a steady handshake, can smile, and start with a positive conversation. If they were late for you, how can you trust that they will be on time for your customers?

Did they dress to impress?
How was their appearance? Did they dress the part or were they disheveled? This is another big one for me; you do not get a second chance at a first appearance, and first impressions do count. Is what they wore acceptable attire for a prospective customer? If you have any doubts, the answer is no!

Were they ready to WOW you?
Did they come equipped with a pen and something to write on? Whether it's an old-fashioned portfolio or a new tablet, I don't care, but I do care that they take notes and have questions and information already prepared. Have you ever had someone arrive for an interview with a briefcase and just leave it closed? The better prepared they are, the more I love them.

Did they "go slow to go fast" on research?
I am unimpressed when a candidate has not taken the time to do the research and get to know the company. I have had experiences where I told recruiters that an individual didn't even know the name of our CEO and worse, didn't review the job description prior to the interview. The expectation is that they know the business—what they will be selling, their competitors, and what the role is—or how else will they know if they can be successful?

Can they tell it as it was?

I am always excited to hear clear examples of how they have been successful. Do they really know how to prospect, research, discover, problem solve, and close? If they cannot explain the how, what, when, and where, did they sell it or did someone else? Can they give a client as a reference?

Do they have "big ears?"

Today's successful salespeople listen more than they speak. They are curious, they are hungry to know more about their customer's pain, and they dig deep under the surface. Those who get a clearer understanding of what a customer wants are usually the most successful. A salesperson who just likes to talk is probably going to be mediocre at best.

Are they team players?

You are hiring an individual contributor, but are they a "team player?" I use Jim Collins's "Good to Great" analogy of having the "right people" on the bus and everyone owning a "Big Hairy Audacious Goal" to find out whether the person will work for their success, the team's success, and the business's success. It has to be all three or it will not work for anyone.

Do they love what they do or they just need to work?

Apart from professionalism, attitude, and level of preparedness, one thing I look for is a passion in what they do and what they know. Salespeople who are professional but have no other real tie to the position tend to leave or hide when things get tough. Those with passion come forward with great ideas, they are positive, and they want to contribute not only for their success but also that of others.

A final piece of advice: if they did not WOW you, if you did not feel that you could not let this one go, if you did not think that this one really knew how to win, DO NOT HIRE THEM!

About the Author

Sue Tidswell is a Sales Guru and Staffing Industry Expert, named in 2018 as one of the industry's Top Global 150 Women. Sue's impressive clientele list includes some of the world's largest companies, including Honeywell, Goldman Sachs, Bank of America, British Petroleum, and Pfizer. She has also worked for several Global Staffing Companies that include: ManpowerGroup, Volt, and Randstad and a long-standing career and relationship with RR Donnelley.

Sue's passion is taking her "Practically Brilliant" approach to retaining and acquiring a well-balanced client portfolio, aligning great talent with opportunity. She helps build sales organizations and transform recruiting agencies from mediocre to high-performing engines and increased revenues.

Her focus and business specialties are: creating and developing global and domestic sales teams, operations management, public relations, contract negotiations, revenue building, and client relations.

Sue's hands-on approach and constant contact with the client provides insight for both the customer and her business to win. She seeks out and thrives at accepting challenges, from turning around underperforming sales organizations to the opportunity of building a start-up and delivering groundbreaking results.

AHAthat®

THiNKaha has created AHAthat for you to share content from this book.

➲ Share each AHA message socially:
  http://aha.pub/EffectiveSalesForceHiring

➲ Share additional content: **https://AHAthat.com**

➲ Info on authoring: **https://AHAthat.com/Author**

Sue Tidswell
AHAthat Author

Hey, Did You **AHA**that®?